SEASONS OF THE HEART

SEASONS OF THE HEART

Poems by Mac

Written by:

James (Mac) W. McLauchlan, Jr.

DEDICATED TO:

My daughter Tara, my son James
and their Mother, Sally.

Special thanks to the many waitresses and bartenders,
both in the United States and in Japan, who put up
with me while I worked on this book.

Thank you for reminding me that my glass
was never half empty, but always half full.

The two poems at the end of the book were written
by my Grandfather, Ernie Fraser and by my son,
James W. McLauchlan, III.

TABLE OF CONTENTS

FOR MY DAUGHTER

Whenever the need arises,
Whisper my name to the moon.
I will hear your voice
As it dances among the stars.

If your heart is aching,
Remember holding my hand.
I will float from heaven
And hold your hand against my heart.

On days when life is living hell,
Call my soul from the river.
I will bring October days
To canoe your cares away.

When weakness torments your spirit,
Think of when I stood tall and strong.
My strength is within you,
For eternity it will be.

TOKYO JAMES

Teach your children
Not to fear the unknown.
Embrace it, learn from it,
Knowledge is growth.

Teach your children
To seek out new horizons.
Strive to feel the anguish
Of fear when all alone.

Teach your children
To venture to the edge.
Feel terrified of falling,
Then move to higher ground.

Teach your children
To respect your wisdom.
Then go their own way,
Without fear....GO!

POEM FOR GABRIEL

A grandson arrived
with the birth of Spring.
The time of his life is
like the Sakura seedling
only now emerging from the soil.

Cherry blossoms signify
a rebirth, a new beginning.
Sakura hold a special place
in the hearts of the Japanese.
Our grandson holds that place in mine.

Our grandson will learn
to embrace each moment
as a precious new start.
For each moment in time
is a new flower in bloom.

Gabriel's life will
always be the fragrance
of a cherry tree in bloom.
His will be a life
of beginnings, without ends.

FATE

Tears are never far from falling,
Through the cracks
Of hearts once broken.
Tears of long lost passion,
Are the stars
Of a never ending sky.

A thousand morning suns,
Will not shine as bright
As my love's smile at dawn.
Night never falls on her beauty,
The full moon blushes
When she takes her evening stroll.

Pain is
loves' lifeblood,
The knife that separates
Ones heart from ones soul.
Pain is the torment,
The burning memory
Of what might have been.

Never had a woman's touch,
Pierced my heart
With such passionate fury.
Fate had never been so cruel,
As it was that Autumn day
When it tore our hearts apart.

POEM

Some days life rears its' ugly head.
Clouds cover my mind.
My heart turns to stone.
Love is gone.

You smile at me, the clouds float away.
The stars in your eyes melt the stone from my heart.
Your hand touches mine.
There is Love.

10.20.09

An old beginning to a new day,
Takao-San beckons.
Long lost spirits wander,
Among cedars old as time.

Sunrise is new, yet so old.
As is a child's birth.
The footprints of the mountain,
Speak of ancient battles fought.

Innocent is the new life,
The soft smile of a child.
Takao-San holds the children dear,
And cries for souls long past.

A new day dawns, a baby cries,
The mountain sheds a tear.
'Tis joy Takao-San cries for,
A new life to show the way.

MAKE MY DAY

Optimistic sunlit morning,
Gives way to stormy sorrow.
Afternoon sun scorches the land,
Desire a shadow on the grass.

Another day of stifling heat,
Shadows dance between the clouds.
Evening solitude approaches,
Love becomes a setting sun.

Dusk delivers the daily despair,
Night falls hard upon the soul
Loneliness fuels hopelessness,
Darkness envelopes the earth.

Her smile mimics the sunrise,
An embrace to light the world.
Sunset turns to sunrise,
When her smile made my day.

MOTHER NATURE

Mother Earth still sings,
A song of love for you.
Raindrops fall from clear blue skies,
To cleanse your lovely skin.

Barren lands await me,
Where birds no longer sing.
Relentless sun blisters my skin,
An early taste of hell.

Mother Nature grows flowers,
For your personal perfume.
Tall oaks provide shade,
For you and only you.

Spring, Summer, Autumn, Winter,
Exist in hearts of love.
There are no seasons for those alone,
Just day after endless day.

SOLSTICE

Align the stars with sorrow,
As moonbeams cry out loud.
The death of Spring is upon us,
Mother Nature sheds a tear.
'Tis Natures way.

Her smiling face is sunshine,
Love a laughing sunbeam.
Spring rains are the teardrops
Of flowers destined to die.
Nature's nectar flows.

The longest day is brutal,
Blue skies hide behind the haze.
Summer days bring the end
To the flowers of spring.
'Tis Nature's way.

TERESA

Her smile is a sunbeam
On a windy rain swept day.
Keeping me warm
While cold rain paints my face.

The twinkle in her eye
Is a midnight sunrise.
The Love in her heart
Unchains the loneliness in mine.

Her touch a lovely torment,
Sunshine dancing in the shade.
My heart beats cold,
Her Love a wildfire burning.

The Love she has within her,
Is a rose in bloom.
The Love in my heart
Is the flower of her smile.

TO LOVE A WOMAN

Her smile is a Magnolia
In full Springtime bloom.
Sunlight dancing
In a drop of morning dew,
Is the sparkle in her eyes.

She is a flower petal,
Strong, delicate beauty.
Moonbeams skipping
Across a mountain lake,
Are her flowing hair.

Her face is the sunrise
On a sultry summer day.
Dawn blossoms
With light as soft
As her touch as she awakens.

She is an Autumn sunset,
A cool warmth in the air.
The wood fire burns
With the love
That warms her heart.

A LONG RUN

Long may your love,
Flow through my heart.
May we grow together,
Meet life's sunset hand in hand.
Long may we run.

I live for you alone,
You are my sunrise.
My sunbeam of hope.
Our love will forever
Reach beyond the limits of time.

The days grow short,
Her smile a Summer breeze.
A cool evening wind
Fans a flame of fire in my heart.
Long may it burn.

My life is her love,
Her smile my starlit sky.
Her beauty is the moonlight
Painting delicate flowers
On a mountain lake of Love.

ANOTHER DAY

Sunrise arrives,
'Tis another solemn day.
Love teases in the morning
And fades away at dawn.

Afternoon comes tomorrow,
Another yesterday.
Her heartbeat is mine
And hers' alone.

Evening sunset,
A promise always, never kept.
Her smile is my heart
Breaking with the dawn.

Midnight closes in,
To choke the morning sun.
I held her hand at daybreak,
By morning she was gone.

DISTANT LAKE

A distant lake calls my name,
The mountains play our song.
My true love longs to hold me.
Our hearts are one,
Our lives so far apart.

May the early mountain mist
Conceal us from the pain of loneliness.
A touch of her hand, I am whole.
We are together,
Yet so very far apart.

The morning mountain air
Sings in harmony with the Winter sky.
Her eyes are the sunrise
Shining on the mountain peaks,
Illuminating my heart.

May the rain fall upon me
While sunshine brightens a new day.
Rainbows smile upon me as
My love walks into and out of
My life once again.

EQUINOX

Summer collides gently,
With Autumn's ageless smile.
Dawn brings a chilling warmth,
Nightfall her embrace.

The Equinox approaches,
Days grow short, shadows long.
Evening's silence is broken
By the sound of falling frost.

A warm breeze drifts
Across snow covered leaves.
A hint of Summers' past,
And Winter sure to come.

Her love is my warmth
On this cold Winter morn.
Her touch is a sunrise,
To hold in my hand.

ON THE HILLTOP

High in the hilltops,
Fog clouds the mind from reason.
Thin air transforms intellect
Into random railings
Of the lonely man's soul.

Rain glistens upon the grasses,
Reaching skyward from the plains.
Water cleanses the emotions
Of a one time caring way,
The thirst for love has drowned.

Snowflakes gently fill
The forest's mighty crown.
'Tis a sparkling white prison,
Which confines a smile
That once roamed free.

Wind dries the tears,
Of enduring singularity.
Blowing through the crevice,
Of spirit long since broken,
Twisting desire into emptiness.

Sunshine begets heat,
Flames of passion burning
Through hollow naked hearts.
High on the hilltop they scream
The souls of solitude.

KIREI

Her eyes hold the beauty
Of a thousand morning suns.
The stars in the sky
Are the twinkle in her eye.

She is a red rose
Blanketed by morning dew.
Sunbeams dance in color
All around her.

Her smile is the sunrise
Melting the frost
From the flowers of
Winters long ago.

Her love is a warm Spring day,
Soothing raindrops falling
As the sun shines
Ever so bright on our Love.

MY BEAUTIFUL FLOWER

Cherry blossoms paint the sky,
Her smile paints my heart.
The touch of her hand
Is the flower of Sakura,
Soft, firm and wonderful.

Cherry trees are singing
Songs of Love for me.
New beginnings are dancing
Upon long lost memories.
She is the birth of Spring.

Sakura blossoms put an end
To the cold dreary moments
That occupy a Winter's day.
Her eyes are the beauty
Of the first Sakura in bloom.

Blossoms sing in harmony,
Flowers dance upon the wind.
The most beautiful flower,
My Miha,
Will forever be my spring.

SONGBIRDS

Songbirds sing the blues today,
And all days evermore.
Harmony that never was,
An off key melody.

Early morning heartbreak,
The sunrise sheds a tear.
A symphony of love and life,
A piano out of tune.

Hiding in the morning fog,
Is where her smile resides.
A voice that once was music.
Is now a silent dawn.

Evening sings a song of Love,
Passion plays a tune.
No longer will the starlight,
Sing a song of Love.

A NEW SMILE

A new smile on the horizon.
She looks the other way,
Right at me.
So I walk into the nighttime sun,
She smiles and walks away.

Autumn winds fan flames of passion.
Love moves quickly through the door,
Then strolls on by.
So I stand at the edge of daylight,
To watch the sun set at noon.

A new smile to break my heart.
Her gaze is one of endless love,
She shuts her eyes.
So I walk into a summer snowdrift,
She looks into my soul.

Her touch a warm Spring day in Winter.
Love blooming in the snow,
She runs away.
So I dance upon a frozen lake,
While My Love cries upon her pillow.

BLUE ROSE

Tears of happy sorrow
Once again fill the evening sky.
Sunrise will return,
My love will not.

Love is an Autumn leaf,
Vibrant, full of color.
Beautiful in its' glory
Gone with Winter's kiss.

Cry me out of Winter,
Into Springtime's warmth.
May the flowers of Spring
Bring new life to us all.

Love, tenderly
Breaking my heart again.
A blue rose in her hand,
No love in her heart.

TOMORROW

Love is an emptiness
Of passion's cup overflowing.
The hollow feeling
Of holding a hand not there.

'Tis a helpless feeling
When Love blocks
The sunlight of reason,
When words have no meaning.

Loving her is futile,
Yet loving her is not.
It is a love for always,
A love to end tonight.

The sun will set again today,
And at the morning sunrise
She will show her love to me,
Tomorrow....yesterday.

DREAMING

Another dream haunts the night,
Magical moonbeams warm my face.
The touch of her hand
Warms the sunrise of tomorrow.

Lay down your head my Love,
Let evening flow into night.
My arms will hold you
'Till the song of morning comes.

Daydreams kiss the starlight,
Morning gives birth to daylight.
Her body next to mine
Is yesterday's future.

I will always love you,
Your heartbeat is my life.
To breath is to hold you,
Without you, just a dream.

FALLING STAR

Icicles dancing
On the light of the moon.
A lunar Eclipse is upon us.
The full moon is fading,
As does the Love I once knew.

Stars in the sky
Awaken the moonbeams,
Who dance on my Love's smile.
Earth's shadow moves between us,
Love struggles to survive.

An Eclipse,
The light that was her love,
Is now the darkest night.
Moonlit skies will come again,
Her soft caress will not.

She smiles
When the moon returns.
Her love is moonlight,
Her kiss an evening sky.
She is my falling star.

LOVE LOST

Love lost is something gained,
A beating heart carries love within.
To love a woman
Is to put your hand in the flame
Of the fire of life.

Tho tears obscure my vision,
Her smile is always in my sight.
The diamonds in her eyes
Are never ending sunbeams
To light the darkness in my life.

My sweet Love so far away.
To breath without her
Is to never take a breath.
She is the sunrise in my heart,
The air I breath is her.

NO REASON

Sunset love,
She smiles an empty dream.
No reason
To breath the air of loneliness,
'Tis only sorrow in disgrace.

Dawn beckons,
Night dreams awakened.
No reason
For her to love me,
Reality dressed as a dream.

Afternoon sunshine,
Her eyes torch my soul.
No reason
For the shadow that lingers,
'Tis only love long gone.

Sunrise is dark,
The morning sun is cold.
No reason
To see the sun shine,
Left in the dark again.

THUNDERCLOUDS

Thunderclouds tattoo my mind,
With memories of gentle rain.
Her smile is the rainbow,
Bringing color to my life.

Storm clouds gather,
Lightning scorches my soul.
Her love is a midnight sun,
My heart a lonely sunset.

Rain falls in torrents,
Hail falling from the sky.
Her love, a rose in bloom,
My heart a Winter Tulip.

Rainbows blooming,
'Tis sunrise after the storm.
Morning smiles upon us,
I awaken in her arms.

WARM WINTERS' DAY

Winter slowly creeping
From her icy perch in hell.
Cold winds burn
Like intense Summer sun.

Love blossoms as leaves turn
To lovely shades of bronze.
The leaf of a Japanese Maple
Gives color to my Love's lips.

Retreating Autumn brings
Snow dust to the mountain tops.
The arrival of snow tells the trees
To drop their leaves and surrender.

Cool fall air warms my heart,
Winter's chill a fire burning.
May her touch always be
A warm November day.

BROKEN DREAMS

Sit with me so far away,
Let cold sunshine warm your face.
The heat of your passion
Turns my heart to ice.

Leave me now and hold my hand,
Let my Autumn be your Spring.
May the seeds of your love blossom
Into the flower of my heart.

Together we will grow apart,
As the cold hand of Winter
Slaps down a warm Summer day.
Our Love is one and none.

Look away then smile at me,
Let my sunset be your sunrise.
Summer rains fall once again,
On empty fields of broken dreams.

EMPTINESS

Emptiness fills my being,
Another hollow daybreak.
Her touch is but a memory,
A shadow in the mist.

The promise of her smile,
Fades like a full moon at dawn.
Eyes that held a look of Love,
Now hold a vacant stare.

Morning arrives without her,
I look and she's not there.
Dawn's promise,
Is but a dewdrop in the sun.

Evening draws near,
A cold August night.
Sweat on my brow,
A chill in my heart.

FOREVER IN MY ARMS

The tear in my eye
Holds her reflection in my mind.
Springtime anticipation,
Blooming flowers of Love.

Her touch a gentle Spring rain,
Softly caressing Mother Earth.
An Equinox celebration,
Longer days of Love.

The crack in my heart
Holds a long forgotten memory.
A Springtime love in Winter,
Ice melting from my heart.

She brushes her hair with sunlight,
Bathes in the light of the moon.
She lives in the beauty
Of a clear blue sky.
Forever in my arms.

A SMILE

Cool evening breeze,
A hint of Autumn's approach.
Mountain Columbine blooms,
My Love smiles.

Silent sunset,
Songbirds no longer sing.
The beauty of the day
Grows old.

Soft clouds paint the sky,
Summer reaches a conclusion.
The new moon rises,
Splendid in its' absence.

Dawn arrives lonely,
Another hollow embrace.
A dark starlit night,
Somewhere my Love smiles.

MOUNT TAKAO

An old beginning to a new day,
Takao-san beckons.
Long lost spirits wander
Among cedars old as time.

Each sunrise new, yet so old,
As is a child's birth.
The footprints of the mountain
Speak of ancient battles fought.

Innocent is new life,
The smile of a child.
Takao-san holds the children dear
And cries for those souls lost.

A new day dawns, a baby cries,
The mountain sheds a tear.
'Tis joy the mountain cries for,
A new footprint on her path.

NO SHADOWS

Emotion sails into darkness,
A night devoid of starlight.
Love disappears quickly,
Fog melting from
A mountain lake at dawn.

Her smile, her touch,
A full moon sunrise.
Long nights of lonely afternoons,
Give light to the pain
Of a Winter morning sunset.

Passion is a nighttime sun,
Morning holds no daylight.
To breath is to love her,
She is the warmth
Of a thousand midnight suns.

Ni-gatsu she says,
Sunrise on the morrow.
No more days of empty nights,
Her smile is my starlight,
No shadows on a sunny day.

TO HOLD A RIVER

Heartbreak lives on the doorstep,
Love dances in the street.
My love is standing next to me,
She is oh, so far away.

Hollow is the feeling
Of an empty heart and soul.
Love rises with the sun,
Then fades into the night.

Tears swell the eyes
On a lovely Winter's day.
Another promise broken,
A promise never made.

Rivers flow to the sea,
Love drifts on the current of life.
To capture love is to hold
A river in your hands.

YEAR END

Year end draws near,
Another end to the beginning.
Her smile haunts my being,
Time stands still.

December fading,
Winter warms the coldest hearts
With dreams of Springtime love.
She gazes at me.

A look in her eyes,
A new year, a vision,
Everything becomes clear.
The future, long past, is now.

Fear greets the change
From the old to the new.
Old years never meet their end,
It is always a new beginning.

The seconds on the clock
Turn to minutes.
May the new year grant me the time
To hold her hand in mine.

A STARLIT NIGHT

Long days
Morph into brief moments in time.
The trees are singing
Songs of starlit nights.

Her smile
Is an Autumn mountain breeze.
Mountains are eternity,
Her love forever more.

The lake
Rests in the bosom of the hills.
Galaxies from time since past.
Lay their stars at my love's feet.

Mother Earth
Lends her strength to those who care.
Sow the seeds of friendship
And life will never end.

CROSSROADS OF THE SEA

Crossroads across the sea.
May her smile ride the waves
To my homeland
And brighten my everyday.

Her eyes are the light of my life.
Many miles bear the burden
Of my broken heart.
I long for the twinkle in her eyes.

The distance between us grows.
Halfway 'round the world
I shall go, alone.
Each mile a new heartache.

Our lives touched across the sea.
We met at the crossroads of time.
Her smile will warm me always,
She is the flower of my life.

KAWAGUCHIKO SMILE

A Kawaguchiko smile.
The sparkle in her eyes
Is sunlight dancing
On fresh fallen snow.

Love is the morning fog,
On a silent mountain lake,
Clinging to the water,
Till it fades away with sunrise.

Her smile is my heartbreak.
Love lost in the foothills
Of memories yet to come.
May she hold her hand in mine.

Mount Fuji looks upon us,
Kawguchiko smiles.
Molten lava warms the earth,
My lady warms my heart.

MOUNTAIN

May the mountain air
Cleanse my soul once again.
The spirits of the mountain
Speak as the sunrise is born.

Clouds hover over the essence
Of what once was life.
A beginning of the end
Of the start of something new.

To be touched by
The mountain's strength
Is to touch the birth
Of life itself.

My Love is a snowflake
Kissed by sunbeams
On a crisp Winter's day.
She is my mountain of life.

OLD MUSIC

Old music on the radio.
Harmonious teardrops
Fall like Spring rain.
May I drown in the memory
Of what might have been.

The D.J. plays our song again,
A melody of memories
Ringing in my ears.
Heartbeat was the rhythm,
Love carried the tune.

A song of love that never ends,
Harmony that never was,
A doomed duet.
Her smile haunts me,
My heart beats off key.

A guitar weeps of loneliness,
The singer's voice is gone.
Another song to cry for,
Heartbreak,
In two part harmony.

ROXANNE REMEMBERED

One night the sun was shining
On empty vibrant streets.
A Champaign sunrise,
Her smile captured my heart.

Morning brought confusion,
Her love a fire at dawn.
We dance thru the morrow,
Two hearts as one.

To anticipate the morning
As a child on Christmas Eve.
She will always be with me,
On my ball field of life.

The sun set at noon that day,
Her kiss forbidden fruit.
Tears flowed, two hearts broke,
As we walked away our lives.

TOKYO 2010

So many voices
Speaking in silent harmony.
Passing each other so slowly
As they race against
The clock of life.

A multitude of footsteps,
Going nowhere, everywhere.
Forward and backward
All in one convoluted motion,
While standing oh so still.

Sleeping without rest,
Yet to sleep is to survive
Another day of endless nights.
Humans floating over concrete,
Smiles trying to escape.

Souls moving in and out
Of reality's icy glare.
Walking on the jagged edge of life,
The future is yesterday's promise
Of hope, happiness and despair.

THE SEASONS

Snowflakes fall in Hades,
Spring rains parch the land.
Storms rage on sunlit mornings
Heartbreak reigns supreme.

Rivers running backward,
Snow showers on a Summer's eve.
Time stops, yet never started,
To remember is to cry.

An August freeze is upon us,
Penguins soar from tree to tree.
Roses bloom in snowdrifts,
Her love is my shadow.

Mountain ranges crumble,
Wild flowers from the desert rise.
Ocean waves crash in silence,
Her heart is mine no more.

HOLDING HANDS

Another day screams to a silent end,
Sunset appears, then goes.
Starlight illuminates the pain
Of another desperate night.

Moonlight is wondrous torture,
A chandelier in the sky.
A kiss from a star reminds me
Of the taste of her lips at dawn.

Herald the sunrise with clear skies,
Torrential raindrops fall.
May the rain fall upon my face
And wash away the tears.

Sunrise warms my weary bones,
And chills the blood in my heart.
We held hands in the morning sun,
Yet now we touch no more.

IF ONLY

Her memory,
Floats through my consciousness,
Autumn leaves
Fall quietly from the trees.

No sound,
As the leaves crash to earth.
No noise,
As my heart cracks again.

Her touch,
An ancient aberration,
Passion fades with time,
A warm body in my dreams.

If only,
My tears could cleanse
The sorrow from my soul,
As Spring rains refresh the earth.

Maybe then,
My aching heart could rest,
Content with a future,
Of desperate lonely nights.

THE VOICE OF LOVE

The sound of her voice is Love,
As it echoes through the hills.
Her whisper is the wind,
Elegantly floating amidst the trees.

Her voice conjures memories,
A full moon shining on the past.
To hold her is to hold moonlight,
Embracing moonbeams with my Love.

I hear her when the birds sing,
She speaks when all is silent.
Her language is the wildflowers'
Fresh as dew drops on her lips.

The moonlit night is quiet now,
The voice of love gone dumb.
Once she said, "I love you".
Though now she speaks no more.

AUTUMN'S PAIN

Autumn rain decorates the forest.
Raindrops become tear drops
Falling from the sobbing leaves.
Misting rain washes tears from my face,
Yet cannot cleanse the pain in my heart.

November carries a cold rain,
A chilling wind blows through my soul.
Winter persecutes my mere existence.
What was the inferno of my passion
Is now merely a flicker of flame.

Snowflakes decorate the sunset painted sky,
Warming chilled emotions as they fall.
Snow Angels walk hand in hand,
Love smiles on the frosty land.
Midnight snow is always bright.

Spring's sunshine offers hope anew,
Love blossoms as snowflakes melt.
Alas, Snow Angels lose their wings,
As the devil's heat turns earth to mud.
Spring flowers bloom and die.

FOOTPRINTS IN THE SNOW

Cold wind conjures memories,
Moments of time in the breeze.
Floating fragments of broken dreams,
Crash to earth with snowflakes white.

Cold wind chills a haunted past,
The present is the future.
The future masks the past,
Your footprint is your being.

Tread lightly on the snowflakes,
They will crush, as will your soul.
Icicles form in the empty bosom
Of the heart that loves no more.

Snowflakes are forever singing,
Though sunlight melts the mind.
Futile desires are crushed
By footprints in the snow.

MY LOVE - GONE

The moment she smiles, I am born,
Her breath is my being.
My consciousness resides
In the open arms of her Love.

Her gaze upon me, I am alive,
A look to nurture ones' soul.
She is never ending moonlight,
A deep running river of Love.

He smile is crying, I am sorrow,
Her tears are my emptiness.
A black hole engulfs my heart,
O' Love that might have been.

Her eyes will never see, I am gone.
Emotion fades as if a dream.
Loves' fantasy is dead now,
A river of Love run dry.

REMEMBER ME

Time weighs heavy on the soul,
The clock of life keeps ticking.
No time for smiles,
No time for love,
Yet time for time to end.

Each day a dance with demons,
The sun rises, only to set.
Dark shadows reign,
Clouds block the sun,
Darkness marks the end of time.

Moonlight moves the spirit,
Moonbeams are life evermore.
Dance in starlight,
Waltz through galaxies,
Gaze at the moon from the heavens.

Time is pain personified,
Born to live, only to die.
Bright is the future
In the child's eye,
Death is peace for the old one.

FROZEN FANTASY

Loneliness begets sorrow,
The cold wind whistles
Through the chasms of my heart,
Freezing emotion, caring, desire.
Ice is my being, my soul.

Sorrow is heartache,
Frozen is My Love,
Her touch a distant dream.
Where once was flaming passion,
Cold, dark embers now reside.

Heartache is the cold,
Of a windy Winter's night.
The chill remembers, a long lost embrace.
Icy passion holds no Love,
Frost stifles all desire.

Cold hearts melt not,
Winter sunshine fools the mind,
Twisting Love's emotions
Into frozen fantasies,
Of hearts that ache no more.

LAKESIDE MORNING

Early morning lakeside,
Fog rising with the sun.
Daybreak adorns the horizon,
Sending nighttime to its' grave.

Darkness gives way,
Songbirds awake in tune.
Singing of new beginnings,
Sorrow sings off key.

Virgin morning chill,
Submits to daylight's warmth.
Fog lifting, lake breathing life,
Yet happiness floats away.

Silent is the sunrise,
Future dreams are silenced aloud.
Sunbeams waltz upon the lake,
As emotion bathes, then drowns.

MISSING YOU

The days pass slowly without you
Each minute a millennium.
Glaciers move faster than hours,
I long to see your smile.

The shadow on the sundial is maddening,
Is the sun suspended in time?
The universe is frozen,
My heart aches for your embrace.

The stars in the sky quit shining,
Galaxies go dark.
The earth ceases to spin,
I miss you, my dear, I miss you.

ONE DAY AT A TIME

One day - My frozen heart aches.
Her smile warms my bosom like
Springtime sun warms the earth.

One day - My heart beats again.
Her touch is the wind blowing
Passion through my soul.

One day - She holds me.
Her embrace is a soft summer rain
Caressing the flowers and soothing my mind.

One day - One day at a time.

THE CANDLE

The candle dances in the breeze,
Brightly burning, carrying hope
On the edges of its' flame.
The flame is warmth,
Comfort embodied in its' presence.

The candle brings hope,
To those souls who have lost their way
In the tunnel of darkness called living.
If the flame could speak
It would announce to all who hear,
Live, burn as if there is no morrow.

Shine while you can,
Embrace the warmth, the beauty,
Hold the fire against your breast.
Take hold the devil's heat,
Grasp, with both hands,
The terrifying torch of life.

Feel the pleasure,
Of scalded emotions,
The burning of heartbreaks gone by.
The candle burns,
As if a beating heart,
Only to die as the wick melts away.

The flame of love,
Ceases to flicker,
Warmth fades to nothing,
We are no more.

SHE IS LOVE

Her heart is the morning,
A smile of sunlit
Loveliness.

She knows not my love,
Nor my desire
To hold her hand in mine.

Eternity may die,
My love for her
Will live forever more.

May the Great Spirit
Someday tell her,
She is Love.

ROXANNE

A smoky room,
A chair,
A lady.

The Sake flows,
She smiles,
Blind Faith.

Love burns my heart,
Tortures my soul,
Blind Faith.

Emotions flow like teardrops,
A broken heart that never mends.
Love is gone,
Blind Faith

THE HANDS OF TIME

If I could turn back the hands of time ---
Run the fingers of the clock
Through the gray of my hair,
Roll back the years
To when you offered your soul.

If I could turn back the hands of time ---
Reset the hourglass of your heart.
I would nurture every second
Of your warm embrace,
The sun would rise and never set.

If I could turn back the hands of time ---
I would learn,
I would understand,
I would accept your love.

Now the hourglass no longer flows.

If I could........

WARM ICE

Harsh rain seeking solace,
Winter winds are weeping.
Cold air burns with every breath,
A single snow cloud cries.

Freezing rain attacks the earth,
Warming the breast of the caring.
Pellets of ice in the soul,
Melt emotion evermore.

Snow flakes now colliding,
An avalanche of pearly white.
Crushing all desire
On this cold and lonely night.

Flames of passion descend
Upon hardened, frozen feelings.
The freezing rain finds solace
In putting out the fire.

SUNRISE OF LOVE

Her smile is the sunshine,
On an otherwise bleary day.
A beacon in the darkness,
Enveloping my being.

Her gaze brings comfort,
To a working man's aching bones.
Eyes that whisper, "I love you."
Though now they cannot see.

Her voice is of the angels,
Music dancing from her lips.
Each word a symphony of love,
Alas, she speaks no more.

The touch of her hand is heaven,
Bringing warmth to the heart,
And a chill up my spine.
A touch turned cold forever.

Her embrace is love eternal,
Soothing the wounds of life's torment.
A celebration of the sunrise,
Which my eyes will see no more.

BLUE SKIES CRYING

Blue skies beg songbirds to sing,
Blackbird silhouettes dance among the clouds.
Blue skies set minds adrift,
With thoughts of peace and love.

White clouds float with aimless purpose,
As they caress the summer sky.
Inspiring the dreamers,
Who dare believe in hope.

Forbidding is the dark sky,
Soaring eagles retreat to nest.
Torment fills the stormy heavens,
Passion's lightning is no more.

Gray are the clouds of despair,
Raining rage upon the soul.
Thunder drowns the heartbeat,
Of a love lost long ago.

RAINBOWS

Choking on tears of life,
Tears a lonely river flow.
Her love a silent current,
Soon the Quiet day will come.

Waiting for a smile of death,
A smile of vicious love.
Love me till the end of time,
End my time with love.

Cheerful, labored breathing,
The sun rises, only to set.
May she take from me the morrow,
Along with my last breath.

Peace, my true love gave me,
My tears no longer flow.
The sky explodes with rainbows,
A new love, somewhere is born.

FUTURE GONE BY

Lost among the mountain tops,
A hollow empty feeling.
Far away from future's grasp,
The past still has no meaning.

Sunset, a lone wolf howls,
Fear flows through the soul.
Empty days breed empty years,
The present is but future's past.

Speak to the spirits long ago dead.
Heed their solemn call.
We are never in the present,
'Tis all past and future pain.

Confined among the clouds today,
Love drifts upon the breeze.
The future is but past relived,
A cynical circle of time.

MY LOVE

Her smile is with me always,
A sunbeam shining
On a lonely drifting cloud.
She is daybreak in my heart.

She moves as a quiet river,
Gently flowing beneath the trees.
Caressing the shoreline,
With her never ending grace.

Her presence sings of passion,
A warm embrace at sunset,
A kiss of the morning dew.
She is the air I breathe.

She walks among Earthly Angels,
Bearing comfort,
Bringing warmth,
Drying the tears from my eyes.

BROKEN HEART

The wound still festers,
From love's loathsome arrow.
Pain's tenure will end,
With the last beat of my heart.

Her kiss still rests upon my lips,
Love everlasting - forgone.
Linger in my heart,
O' pain of memory.

The touch of her hand,
A genesis of desire.
'Tis a long lost dream,
A nightmare of the soul.

She dances in my dreams,
Sends moonbeams through my heart.
Alas, the moon is gone now,
Only starless darkened skies.

A WINTER LIAISON

Winter's wind caressed her hair,
The frigid night attacked.
Lamp posts dressed in lighted swirls,
Danced along the street.

In my arms, we strolled the boulevard,
Together for an instant.
Strangers, united in a lonely land.
Cold of body, warm of heart.

Her presence warmed the night,
Melting old memories.
A girl of a woman, she was,
Awash in frozen flames of desire.

Her embrace stirred long lost passion,
A flash of time remembered.
When love still wandered
Through the cracks of a broken heart.

'Twas a dream

THE FORGOTTEN LOVE

Miles traveled mean nothing,
Hands that held, touch no more.
Bear my children, commandeer my heart,
Sentence me to sorrow.

Your smile brought me comfort,
Smile now and my eyes do cry.
The fire rages against the freeze,
Love's embers smolder, not to die.

A day with no beginning,
Sunset is eternal.
No morning kiss for this one,
A hollow hug to greet the night.

Wonderful and painful,
Please stay and go away.
Pave my heart with memories,
Of kisses in the night.

ARCTIC LOVE

Icicle teardrops,
Frozen emotions burn within.
Sunset brings a happy sorrow,
A smiling discontent.

Winter's tears are painful,
Frostbite for the soul.
A chilling warmth at sunrise,
The wail of joyous pain.

Cold is the heart,
That burns with muted love.
Desire melts the mountain tops,
Yet glacier ice prevails.

May Love die
In the warmth of Winter's glory.
Under cover
Of fresh fallen snow.

SUMMER SUN

The summer sun is ruthless,
Yet she toils with a smile.
Beads of sweat on her forehead
Are her diamonds, she is lovely.

The heat knows no rest,
She swims in the soil, but tires not.
Shirt dark with sweat,
Her soiled face smiles, she is beauty.

Her back aches, hands are sore,
She has nurtured her soul with the earth.
The essence of life is understood,
A woman for the ages.

TOMORROW'S PROMISE

Glorious midday sunshine,
Submits to raindrops falling.
Deceit blankets the earth,
The fire of life is cold.

Soothing summer sunset,
A peaceful evening breeze.
The morrow carries promise,
Friendship, life and love.

Reality rises at midnight,
Tomorrow never comes.
To breathe is not to live,
No love, no life, no being.

Anticipation turns to sorrow
Another sunrise telling lies.
False hope nurtures torment,
Darkness slays the sky.

Early morn holds promise,
'Till the rainbow disappears.
Storm clouds rule the heavens,
Blue skies are nevermore.

RIVER OF TEARS

Tears flow like a canyon river,
Rushing through chasms of solitude.
Icy water, cold like the blood
Which flows through my heart.

The lonely lake of sorrow past.
Awaits the river of tears.
The river carries long lost dreams
To the lake in which they drown.

River snaking down the mountain,
Its' current sweeping away desire.
Love sinks into the icy depths,
The river cries for thee.

SING TO ME

Sing to me O' sweet smile,
Sing a song of sunshine past.
Kiss me sunbeam,
Kiss me as my Love once did.

Her touch a tortured treasure,
Tearing apart my soul.
Hold me like a baby,
Squeeze me like you care.

Look at me O' lovely eyes,
The loving look of hate.
Kill me with your gaze,
And love me with your eyes tonight.

Escort me into Death's abyss,
Hum me tunes of hellfire.
Kiss me one last time,
And let me die in pain.

THE CHILDREN

The beginning of the end,
Or the end of the beginning?
To crave another sunrise,
Or long for final sunset?

Children smile upon me,
'Tis time to go, or not.
Life has lost its' meaning,
Yet the children cry for more.

Pain personifies my being,
Each breath a tortured task.
Curse the early morning,
Damn the light of dawn.

Leave with the wind O' sorrow,
Stand by me children of hope.
Although I shall be gone someday,
My strength will always be.

NECTAR

'Tis cold on this midsummer's eve,
An arctic frost envelopes me.
What once was unbridled passion,
Is now frostbite of the soul.

She kissed me on a summer day,
Held me like no other.
Our love a clear blue sky in June,
The sun would never set.

Cool evening burst into flames,
A warm breeze carries a chill.
What once was fertile ground for love,
Is sterile, void of life.

She held my hand at sundown,
Sweet nectar was her kiss.
Love was for eternity,
'Tis cold this midsummer's eve.

AUTUMN FALLING

Another Autumn falling,
Winters' frost rests upon the trees.
How can the warmth of Summer end,
When Springtime never came?

Love blossoms in the Springtime,
Only to wilt with Summer's heat.
Flowers long since ceased to bloom,
In the garden of the heart.

Summer smiles upon me,
Sunshine sears my aching flesh.
Spring's flowers turn to ash,
Winter preys upon my soul.

Another Autumn falling,
Into Winter's icy lair.
The avalanche is upon me,
Spring will be no more.

THE FLOWER

A single flower,
Emerges from a Springtime snow.
Sunbeams dance with snowflakes,
Flower petals kiss the sky.

A single heart,
Frozen in the hellfire of winter,
Yearning for the warmth of Love,
Breaks in the chill of loneliness.

The flower is life,
A newborn with hope eternal.
Mother Earth's beauty personified,
The flower is love.

The silent heart,
Has fulfilled its' painful destiny.
Sunbeams cease to dance,
This Spring no flowers bloom.

WHISPER

The sun shines brightest when she smiles.
The clouds all fade away.
My tears will be raindrops,
On an otherwise beautiful day.

Her eyes are timeless beauty,
Soft pools of endless love.
My eyes see only darkness,
Midnight at new moon.

Her voice an angel's melody,
"I love you" was the tune.
Tortured silence owns me now,
A whisper on the wind.

SING

Sing me songs O' great one,
Sing me songs to ease the pain.
My heart no longer hears the tune,
Of lovebirds in the Spring.

Play me a tune O' raincloud,
Soft raindrops on flowers sweet.
Thunder me a tune of sorrow,
The rain no longer falls.

Sunrise serenades the morning,
The glowing warmth of love.
My love is an eclipse,
A light that shines no more.

Springtime sings a song of love,
For those who still believe.
Winter's song is evermore,
For those whose love is gone.

CRYING

How can she make me cry today,
Her smile, so long ago.
A thousand years her love since died,
Warm bosom turned to ice.

How can she make me cry tonight,
When our passion burned as one.
If only tears could wash away,
Reminders of what was.

I cried when we were happy,
I cried when we were sad,
I cry each time I hear her voice,
I cry each time she smiles.
I will cry,
I will cry,
Forevermore.

BIRTHDAY

Grayish white snowflakes floating
Amidst the darkened skies,
Cause the mind to wander.

A day of family,
A day to remember,
A time to cry.

The day has past,
Never to return.

LOVE FORBIDDEN

Today is the first day,
Approaching the last day of my life.
Carry my soul across the frozen landscape,
Bathe my passion in ice filled streams.

The Earth warms,
Glaciers melt with a vengeance.
My heart is an iceberg thawed only by her touch.
Her scent is of Spring flowers in bloom.

Raindrops of Love,
She smiles while I cry.
Tortured by her beauty, smitten by her smile.
She is my Love, she is lost in space.

REAPER

Cold rain, angry wind
On this Autumn twilight's eve.
Sunshine is foreign,
Warmth, for those with love.

Heart barely beating,
A chill permeates my being.
The reaper holds my soul
In his cold, soft hands.

Breathing is such pain,
Futile is the effort
Of a beating broken heart.
A lonely trumpet plays.

Hope springs eternal,
In the land of fairy tales.
Her embrace everlasting,
Two hearts live as one.

Reality rains upon
The desolate remains of dreams.
Desire ripped from emotion.
The reaper wins again.

THE PATH

Creatures of the forest
Lie in hiding.
The path is silent,
Step after empty step,
The years approach sunset.

The lonely path
Opens its' long arms,
Enveloping those,
Who dare wander
Into life's abyss.

The path leads nowhere,
Yet reaches all destinations.
Dreams of hope, on hilltops,
Are dashed to pieces,
In the valley below.

The path of warmth and sunshine
Begs songbirds sing aloud.
Life's Autumn leads to Winter,
The path is silent,
Songbirds no longer sing.

SHINING STAR

She flies like a comet.
Traversing the heavens,
Gliding through galaxies,
Sailing into my life.

Her eyes are starlight
On a clear Summers' night.
Warming the sky,
Melting my heart.

Light years away, her star shines.
Growing brighter,
Moving closer,
My shining star.

CLOUDS

The soft blue sky
Frames a lonely white cloud.
Sunshine smothers my mind
And burns the depths of my soul.

Autumn days grow short,
As does the time for love.
The lonely cloud is two now,
Two lost souls in an empty sky.

The October sun sets,
Flowers force a final bloom.
Clouds take on vibrant color,
Flames ignite the Autumn sky.

Fire in the evening sky,
Two clouds burn as one.
Passion, to warm our bodies
'Till Springtime comes again.

THE NIGHT

Moon floating on a flood of tears,
Sleeplessness sings in harmony with sorrow.
Singing the blues with the sandman,
While awaiting the birth of the morn.

Nightmares of lonely love lost.
Fate dreams as destiny trembles,
Fulfilling a prophecy of solitude.
Moonlight is always cold at dusk.

The dawn screams in a whisper,
Sunrise weeps for the empty soul.
Daylight approaches with menace,
No one to speak, no one to care.

A rising sun nurtures emotion's flame,
Lovers embrace, as sunbeams bless the day.
Blue sky, the sandman shivers still,
For some, nighttime never ends.

NO MORE

Take my mind to galaxies afar,
Send my soul to points uncharted.
Release the pain of her memory,
Into the never ending sky.

Torture me with what might have been,
Deliver my desire to the devil.
Cast my heart into the hellfire,
To burn 'till eternity ends.

Drown my love in starlight,
The waning moon a long lost kiss.
Rip the broken heart in two,
Cast the pieces to the wind.

MAKE ME SAD

Make me sad, make me sad,
Pierce me, O' pain of passion lost.
Make me sad, make me sad,
Sing me sad songs today.

Make me cry, make me cry,
Let loneliness linger forever.
Make me cry, make me cry,
The music plays no more.

Make me sad, make me sad,
Hold my hand and hurt my heart.
Make me sad, make me sad,
Forget my final heartbeat.

Make me cry, make me cry,
Memories of misery.
Make me cry, make me cry,
May there be no tears tomorrow.

TWENTY FIVE

Sing to me slowly,
Let the tears flow through my veins.
May the sunset crash upon me,
May the moonlight torch my soul.

Cry with me my dear one,
Sing lonely songs of love.
Sunrise is no more for me,
Only darkness within the dawn.

May your voice be the music,
Of fond memories turned black.
The sun never sets on your beauty,
The sun never shines on my heart.

Years float by with a vengeance,
Time silences all song.
Yet sunset seems to sing to me,
A song of love now gone.

PRINCESS STARLIGHT EYES

My spirit belongs to the sky.
My body is the earth.
My mind is nurtured by the sun.
My heart···
My heart belongs to the starlight.

Her eyes illuminate the darkest forest.
The sparkle in her eyes is greater than all
The stars in the heavens on a moonless night.
My heart···
Her starlight eyes - own my heart.

TRUE LOVE

Her smile, priceless beauty,
Uninhibited by her charm.
A sensuous naiveté,
First flower of Spring.

Her presence, morning sunlight,
Brilliant, yet subdued.
She is the warmth of my being,
A sunset on the plains.

Her embrace, is fire burning,
A white hot flame of love.
Joyful in her passion,
Rain showers bring her smiles.

Her tears, sweet nectar,
To nurture my lonely soul.
Midnight's moon arrives at dawn,
Her love, her smile are mine.

THE PRAIRIE

Sunrise warms the hearts,
Of lovers hand in hand.
Strolling through a prairie
Moistened by early morning dew.
Love blossoms,
As do the flowers beneath their feet.

Soft summer sunbeams,
Waltz with prairie grasses.
Two hearts dancing together
As fires of passion burn their souls.
Love reborn,
Like flowers in their Springtime glory.

Sunset chills the lonely,
Emptiness fills the day.
To wander aimlessly
Through prairies of long lost love.
Is to be a flower,
Wilting in the summer heat.

EAGLE

An eagle soars through clear blue skies,
Worries sail away on the breeze.
I sing the blues with the blue sky,
Clouds block the sun as teardrops fall.

Contentment hides within the soul,
Remember love that was.
Howling winds and broken hearts,
Turn blue sky into thunder.

Painful passion in a cold heart stirs,
Love's warmth a moonlit memory.
My love is the morning fog,
Fading away with daylight's warmth.

Twilight skies are darker,
Than a cloudy sky at noon.
She held my hand under blue skies,
Now the eagle flies alone.

SNOW DAY

White ice in all its' beauty
Covers the world in my view.
Trees draped in highlights of
Delicate snow flakes,
Tell the story of snowfalls past.

Sunlit sparkles dance
From branch to branch,
They illuminate the frozen sky.
The warmth of the scene
Contradicts the frost on my breath.

Sunshine comes, the trees become bare.
Gary skies bring a chill
To match the cold in my heart.
My soul is a leafless tree,
On this quiet, frigid day.

LOVE'S FIRE

Love, the essence of one's being,
Without, we exist no more.
Hollow is the heartbeat,
Void of a caring touch.

We must caress Love's fire to live,
Spent embers are the lonely.
Unending is the torment,
Of heartbreak to the soul.

Love dies upon the sunset,
Sunrise is dark without her.
The love that took my breath away,
Now chokes me in its' absence.

Love, the nectar of life,
Slips away so slowly.
Love's fire fades and dies,
The ashes are so very cold.

MAKE MY DAY

Optimistic sunlit morning,
Gives way to stormy sorrow.
Afternoon sun scorches the land,
Desire a shadow on the grass.

Another day of stifling heat,
Shadows dance between the clouds.
Evening solitude approaches,
Love becomes a setting sun.

Dusk delivers the daily despair,
Night falls hard upon the soul.
Loneliness fuels hopelessness,
Darkness envelopes the earth.

Her smile mimics the sunrise,
An embrace to light the world.
Sunset becomes sunrise,
When her smile made my day.

BROKEN

Too tired to think,
Too tired to breathe.
Each breath a labored legacy,
Foreboding life's last gasp.

Consciousness drifts away,
Awake while sleeping again.
Heavy eyelids will not open,
'Tis time for eternity's sleep.

Heartbeat racing slowly,
The pain forever lasts.
A broken heart will never heal,
Its' destiny to fade and die.

Time moves along so slowly now,
Faint are voices from above.
The darkened sky is bright now,
The final sun has set.

OLD TO YOUNG

The birthday girl is singing,
Songs of life and future triumphs.
The birthday boy has gone away,
Janis and Jimi sing for him now.

Treasure each day, O' birthday girl,
Praise the sun, it rises for you.
Loath the sunrise O' aged man,
May the sunset bring no dawn.

Time is yours, O young one,
Waste it and use it wisely.
Too soon the hourglass will empty,
Eternity will vanish.

You will always be my birthday girl,
More lovely than the Autumn leaves.
The beauty of an October morn,
Is matched only by your smile.

AUGUST 20

Time is infinite, yet finite,
Eternity shall end.
Years become months,
Months days, days hours.

The clock inches backward,
Futures' life undetermined.
Each moment special,
Minutes escape, forever gone.

The hourglass nears empty,
Sand falls to its' silent death.
A new day may dawn,
An old day disappears.

The sundial casts its' shadow,
Dusk gives way to darkness.
Sunrise a long lost memory,
Time has taken its' last breath.

SUNSET

Pain rules the daytime,
Melancholy overtakes the night.
Dawn is not forthcoming,
The moon no longer shines.

Sunrise must be somewhere,
Illumination cries for freedom.
We bask in the darkness,
Brilliant shades of black.

The shadow of death is upon us,
Yet no light for a shadows birth.
Even in the blackened depths,
A fleeting flash of light.

Sunrise carries hope,
Of prairie flowers in bloom.
Yet hope is torn asunder,
By a perpetually setting sun.

JODY

The following was written by
my Grandfather, Ernie Fraser,
about my sister Jody McLauchlan.

Jody was a March of Dimes poster girl.

Hello world, I am Jody
The March of Dimes girl.

Now will you please listen,
For out there in the disten.
There is a dim light that can glow.

For that we all know,
That no one can help everyone,
But everyone can help just someone.

To help make that dim light shine
Please give to the March of Dimes.

Now from just a few,
I am Jody saying, Thank You.

A poem by my son, James W. McLauchlan, III

LIVING IN THE COUNTRY

To watch the sun set, over a blanket of soybeans
Swaying in the cool evening breeze. To see the
Harvest Moon, glowing orange, bright as all the
Stars in the sky, and the reflection of it all over
A clear, placid lake of deep blue complexion.
The brisk smell of pine trees in the morning
Air; how there is always one lonely goose in
The back of the huge, honking V, as they make
The long trek south for the icy winter. And the
Howl of the hungry coyotes, heard for miles
Around in the middle of a calm, cool night; the
Way the crystal white snow blankets the peaceful
Earth as far as the eye can see; and the storms,
Wind racing over hills and against the tall oak trees,
The rain not falling down, but riding the wind as it
Glides sideways across the fields; the thunder roaring
Like a hundred drums, beating in the same motion
Of blistering noise, and the lightning, bolting across
The sky like an orange, flaring rocket of zigzag flight.
My home.